Moving and Growing

By the end of this book you will know more about:

- Bones.

- Skeletons.

- Muscles.

- How animals move.

You will:

- Do a survey.

- Use Fact Files, books, CD-ROMs and the Internet for research.

What are you like inside?

Nicola and her friends were discussing what their bodies were like inside and talking about how they moved.

We need food and drink because on the television you see marathon runners drinking pop and eating chocolate.

We have blood inside our body. It helps us move.

We need to have a firm shape to move, a bit like a bicycle frame.

⭐ What are your ideas?

⭐ What do you think is inside your body that gives you your shape?

⭐ Draw on Task Sheet 1 what you think give your body its shape.

⭐ Add to it your ideas about how you move your body.

Animals can move in different ways.

Animals on the move

 Why do you think animals move?
Here are some different ways
that animals move:

crawl   **hop**   **run**   **swim**   **walk**   **fly**

Match the animal to the way of moving.
Make a table like this:

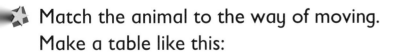

Animal	Way of moving
Frog	

⭐ **Humans and some other animals have skeletons inside their bodies. Skeletons are made of bones.**

Skeletons

💥 Many animals have a skeleton.

💥 Think about what a skeleton is.

> Where do you think your skeleton is?
>
> What do you think it is made of?

A dinosaur skeleton

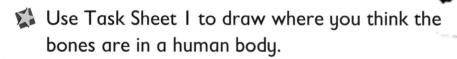

💥 Use Task Sheet 1 to draw where you think the bones are in a human body.

💥 Think about what shapes your bones are and show these on your drawing.

💥 Share your drawing with others. How could you find out what shapes your bones really are?

4

YOU NEED:

very large piece of paper

marker pen or crayon

Extra Challenge

 Put a very large piece of paper on the floor. One person lies on the paper.

Someone else draws around that person to make a big outline drawing of their body. Now feel the different bones in your body. Where is the skull?
What does it feel like?
Draw the skull on the diagram. Next to the diagram, write a word that describes the skull, such as hard or round.
Feel the bones in your arms. How many bones can you feel?
Draw some arm bones on your diagram.
What other bones can you feel?

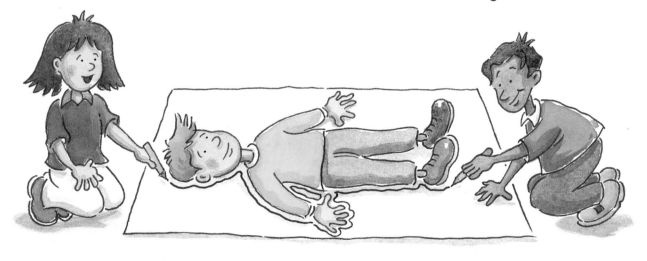

Take turns to label your outline drawing.

Try to draw and label these bones on your picture:

ribs	backbone	shoulder
hip	forearm	wrist
hand	fingers	thigh
kneecap	shin	ankle
foot	toes	

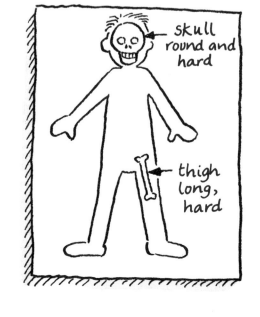

5

Using X-rays to see our bones

We cannot normally see our skeletons. But doctors sometimes use a machine that takes special photographs of the inside of our bodies. These photographs are called X-rays. They show our bones.

 Look at these X-rays.

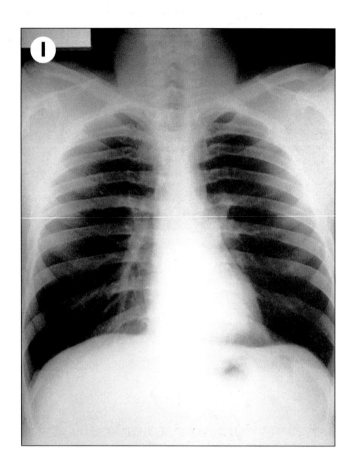

1

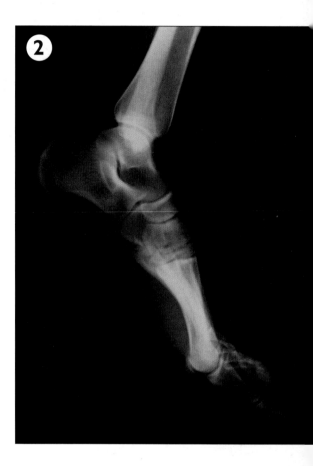

2

Words to learn and use:
skeleton
skull
X-ray

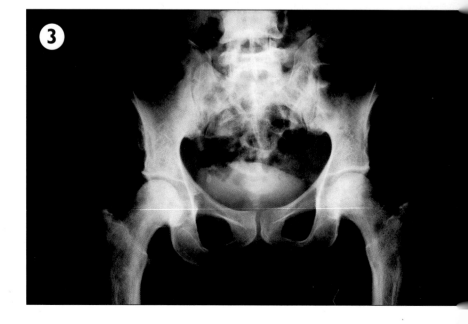

3

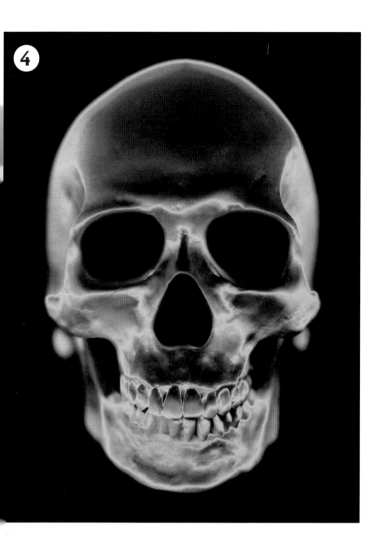

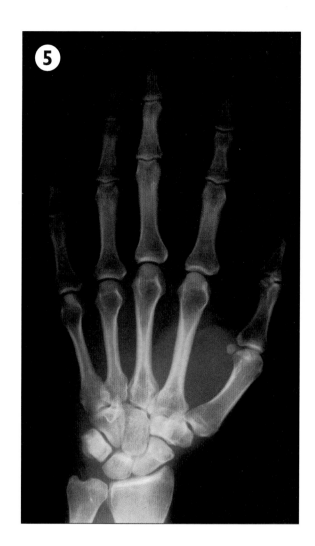

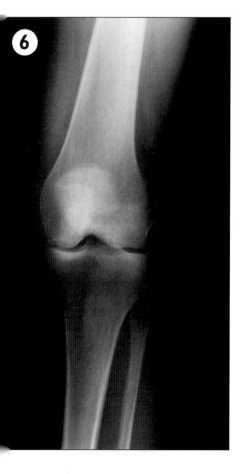

⬥ Make a table listing the bones shown on each X-ray.

X-ray number	Bones
1.	
2.	
3.	
4.	
5.	
6.	

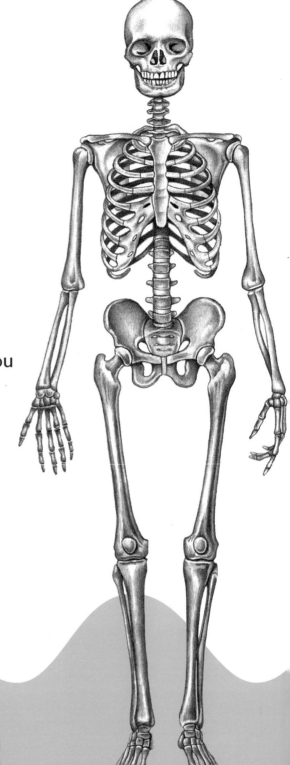

Look at this picture of a human skeleton. This is what your skeleton is like. Is it like your drawing in Task 3?
What is the same about your drawing and this picture?

 With a partner, see how many bones you can name on this skeleton picture. Look at the list of bones on Task Sheet 2 and draw lines from each bone to the place where you would find it on the skeleton.

Fact File

Your skeleton:

- is inside your body.
- gives you shape and stops you wobbling like a jelly.
- is made of bone.
- has three main parts:
    1 a head, spine or backbone with a rib cage;
    2 leg and arm bones;
    3 shoulders and hips.
- has muscles attached to bones.
- protects important parts of your body such as the heart and brain.

Other animal skeletons

3

You can find out about other animal skeletons using books, models, CD-ROMs, and the Internet. Some museums have collections of animal skeletons that are worth visiting.

The dinosaurs were some of the biggest animals that ever lived on Earth. Dinosaurs are now extinct, but their skeletons are sometimes found preserved in the ground. By carefully digging them out and studying them, scientists can make models of dinosaur skeletons.

 Look at this picture of a dinosaur skeleton.

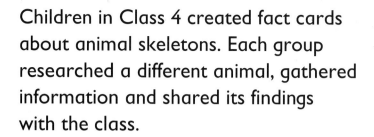

Fact card

Name: Tyrannosaurus

How to say it: Ti-ran-oh-sore-us

Where it lived: North America

Mass: 10,000 kilograms

Length: 14 metres

Height: 6 metres

Food: Other animals

When it lived: 70 million years ago

Number of legs: 4

How it moved: walked on 2 legs

Other details about its skeleton: massive skull

This is what Tyrannosaurus looked like.

Children in Class 4 created fact cards about animal skeletons. Each group researched a different animal, gathered information and shared its findings with the class.

One group made a fact card about a dinosaur called **Tyrannosaurus**.

They found out how to say its name, where it lived, how it moved, how big it was and what it ate.

This is what their fact card looked like.

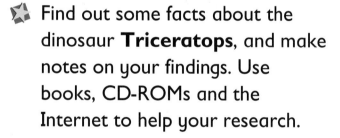 Find out some facts about the dinosaur **Triceratops**, and make notes on your findings. Use books, CD-ROMs and the Internet to help your research.

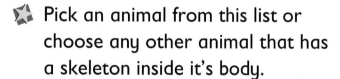 Pick an animal from this list or choose any other animal that has a skeleton inside it's body.

grey heron

killer whale

python

pike

giraffe

Stegosaurus.

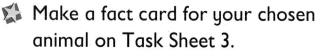 Make a fact card for your chosen animal on Task Sheet 3.

Python

Killer whale

Observe, compare and describe different bones.

Comparing skeletons

....

 Look at these pictures and compare the two skeletons.

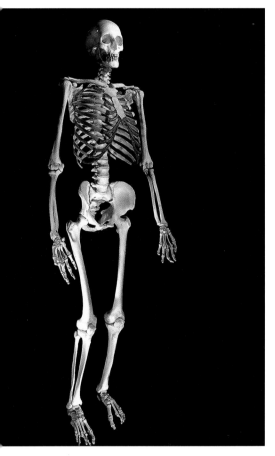

Human skeleton

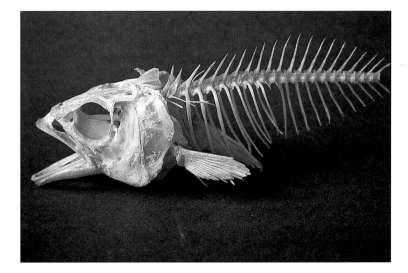

Fish skeleton

When Class 4 compared a dog and a human skeleton, the children began by asking some questions such as:

Do dogs have a skull like humans do?

How is a dog's skeleton like our skeleton?

How is a dog's skeleton different to our skeleton?

Our questions	Our answers
1. How is this skeleton like our skeleton?	
2.	

Now try asking some questions about fish and human skeletons, or about two other animal skeletons chosen from different fact cards.

List the answers to your questions then make a table showing clearly your questions and answers.

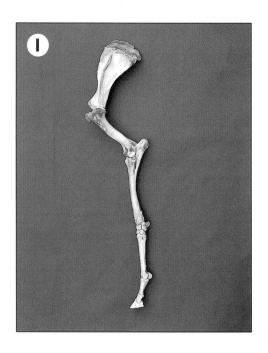

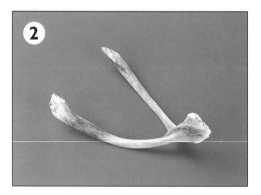

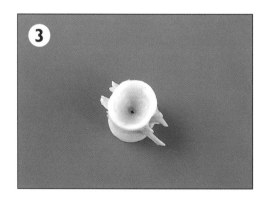

 Task **8** *Funny bones*

Look at the photographs of bones from a **horse**, a **fish**, a **chicken** and a **dog**.

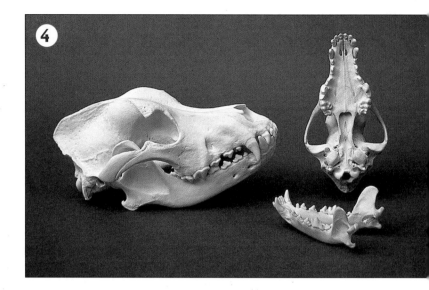

Match the photograph of bones to the correct animal.
Does your group agree with you?

Think of some words to describe:

- What each bone looks like.

- What **properties** each bone has.

Draw a picture of each bone and make a table for comparing your findings.

Animal	Bone	What it looks like	Properties
fish	bone from spine	round, hollow in middle, several ridges and projections; quite small	small, hard, light, knobbly

Which animal bones do you think are stro▮
Which are brittle? Which are smooth?

Broken bones

Some animals, including humans, can
break their bones.

 Look at this X-ray of an arm.

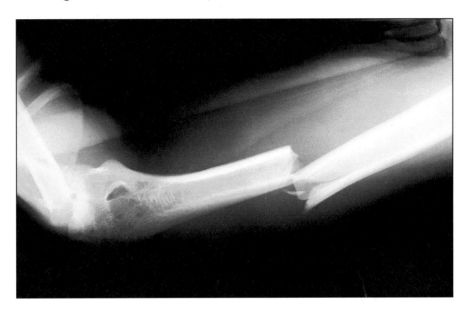

 What's wrong with the arm?
How can you tell? Which bone is broken?

Extra Challenge

 Carry out a survey at home and in school, to
collect information about people who have
broken a bone. Ask questions like these:

Which bone did you break?
How old were you when you broke it?
How did you break it?
Where were you when you broke your bone?

 What do your results tell you? Use these
questions to help you.

• Which bones do people break most often?

• Do most people break bones when they are
at primary school, secondary school or after
they have left school?

Bones and growth

Your skeleton was growing inside your body before you were born. Look at the pictures showing the skeleton of a baby and an adult.

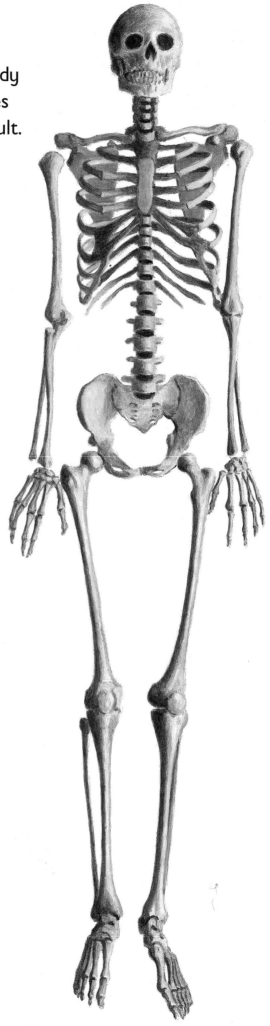

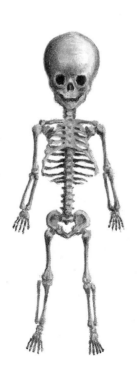

- Which is the baby's skeleton?

- How do you know?

- Which is the adult's longest bone?

- Which part of the adult skeleton has grown the least?

**Plan and carry out a survey.
Show your findings in a table,
bar chart or pictogram.**

Scientific Enquiry

Task 1

Bone survey

....

4,5

✶ Think of some questions to investigate
about the size of bones.

For example:

Do boys have longer arms than girls?

*Do Year 6 children have longer arms than
Year 4 children?*

✶ Use the planning board on Task Sheet 4 to
plan your investigation. It has been started
to help you.

✶ Use Task Sheet 5 to make a bar chart of
your results.

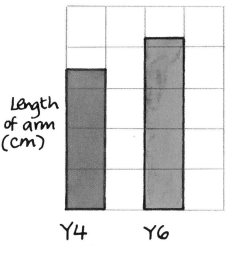

Our graph showing
length of arm in 10 Y4
and 10 Y6 children

Length
of arm
(cm)

Y4   Y6

Classes used in survey

✶ What does your evidence show?
How could you make this
investigation better?

✶ Make up some questions about your
evidence that others can answer using the
table of results and bar chart.
Make sure you can answer the questions
you ask. Try them on another group.

How do worms support themselves?

Animals like humans, birds, frogs, snakes, and fish have skeletons inside their bodies. They all have a backbone or spine made of several small bones joined together. Each small bone is called a **vertebra**. Animals with backbones are known as **vertebrates**. Some animals don't have a spine. They are called **invertebrates**. Many invertebrates, such as earthworms, jellyfish and slugs have very soft bodies. Some invertebrates, such as insects, crabs and limpets have a hard skeleton on the outside.

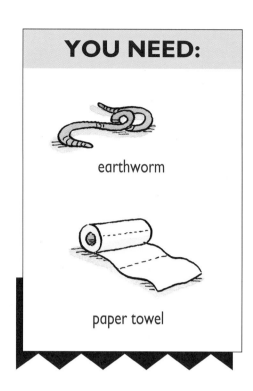

YOU NEED:

earthworm

paper towel

Slug

✸ Put an earthworm on a paper towel. Watch and feel it moving. How does it move its body? Can you hear it moving?

✸ Try to observe some of these invertebrates.

Beetle

Crab

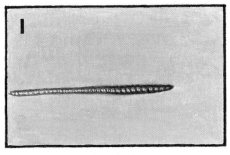

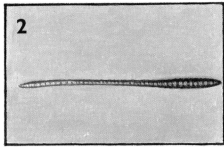

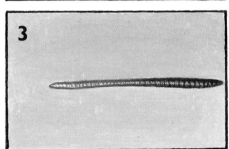

✦ Look at the pictures of a worm taken by Class 4 using a digital camera. How does the worm move?

⚠ *Wash hands after handling animals. Treat them carefully and put them back where they came from.*

✦ Use reference books, CD-ROMs and the Internet to research some animals that don't have a bony skeleton. How are they supported? There are many invertebrates to choose from including caterpillars, flies, slugs, snails, worms, octopuses and starfish.

Why do these animals feel soft?

Fact File

Muscles

- Muscles are joined to bones.
- Muscles make bones move.
- Muscles work in pairs.
- Muscles can shorten or **contract** and stretch or **relax**.
- When a muscle contracts it pulls the bone to which it is joined and the bone moves.
- Muscles use energy from food to contract. We say contraction is **active**.
- Muscles need much less energy when they are relaxed. We say relaxation is **passive**.

Muscles move bones by working in pairs.

 Task **13** *Muscle power*

Nicola and her friends decided to see who had the strongest grip.

They made a hand grip tester using the equipment.

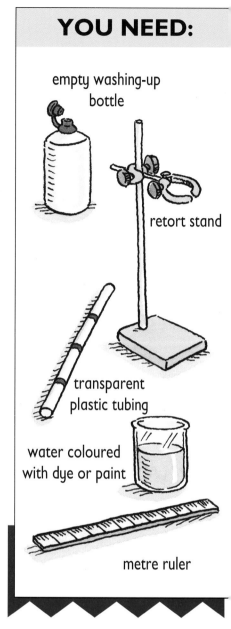

YOU NEED:

empty washing-up bottle

retort stand

transparent plastic tubing

water coloured with dye or paint

metre ruler

✴ Make your own grip tester.
Plan how you will record the results.

✴ Who has the strongest grip?

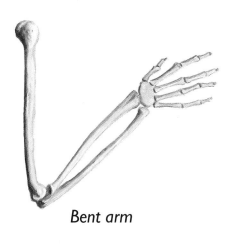

Bent arm

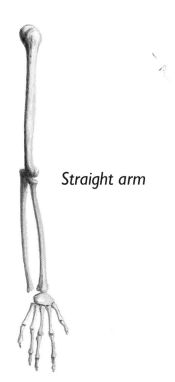

Straight arm

Muscle quiz

- Feel the muscle in the front of your arm when it is bent.
  What does the muscle feel and look like?
  What is this muscle doing to bend the arm?
  Is this muscle now active or passive?

- Straighten your arm.
  What does the muscle feel and look like?
  What is this muscle doing now your arm is straight?
  Is this muscle now active or passive?

- Try it again, this time feeling the muscle at the back of the arm.
  How do muscles move the arm?

- Draw two diagrams to show how muscles bend and straighten your arm. Think about how they work in pairs - one muscle contracting as another relaxes. Write on each diagram to show whether the muscles are relaxed or contracted, active or passive.

Extra Challenge

- Find out the names of the muscles that move the arm.

- Muscles in other parts of your body are used for movement.
  Make a table like this one to show what other muscles do.

Muscles	What they do
face muscles	allow smiling, biting and chewing food
muscles on spine	
muscles of leg	
muscles of neck	
muscles between ribs	

Exercise makes muscles work hard and this is good for you.

Task 15 *Muscles and exercise*

You use muscles to move. When you exercise you breathe more deeply and more quickly. This brings more oxygen into your body. Your muscles need more oxygen and more food such as sugar when you exercise. Blood takes food and oxygen to the muscles. Food and oxygen give the muscles energy to move.

★ Think about what your body feels like when you have exercised hard in games or P.E.

★ Think about what your body feels like when you are resting. Compare how you feel. Look at the picture showing what it can feel like to exercise hard.

Words to learn and use:
contract
exercise
invertebrate
property
relax
spine
support
vertebrate

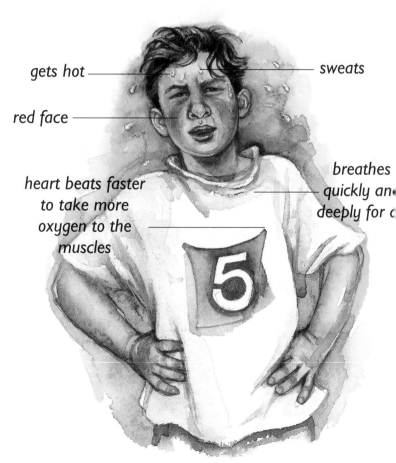

gets hot — — sweats

red face —

heart beats faster to take more oxygen to the muscles —

breathes quickly and deeply for c

This is Jason. He has just run a 100 metres sprint race.

★ Draw and write to show how Jason will feel when he has rested after exercise.

★ Remember exercise can strengthen muscles and is very good for your health.

Scientific Enquiry

Investigating skin temperature

6

Jason and his friends decided to investigate their skin temperature, to see if it increased after exercise.

This is their planning board:

YOU NEED:

temperature sensor or digital thermometer

Our question: Does the temperature of your hand increase after exercising hard?

Our prediction:
We think the skin will get hotter.

What we will do: We will take the temperature of the skin on the hand before exercise and straight after running around the school field.

We will use:
A temperature sensor and a computer or digital thermometer.

We will record our results using a table like this.

	Highest temperature °C
Before exercise After exercise	

Make your own enquiry by following Jason's plan. Make your own planning board on Task Sheet 6.

What do your results tell you?

Checkpoint 1

Concept map

Look back through your work. Make a concept map using these words:

skeleton   body   bone   move   support   muscle   contract

exercise   tired   hot   human   worm   snail   grow

Join as many words as you can like this.

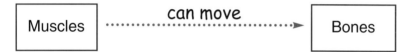

Muscles ········ can move ········> Bones

Checkpoint 2

Make up a Wordsearch

7

Make a wordsearch about moving and growing, for your friend.

Choose some of the words on Task Sheet 7 and write them in the grid of squares. You can write them in any direction - across, up, down or diagonally.

Fill empty squares with any letters.

Cut out the wordsearch and swap with your friend.

Draw a ring around any words you spot.

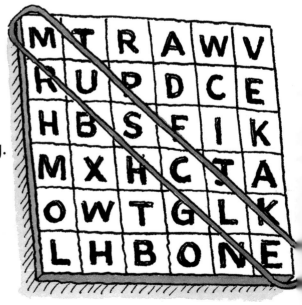

Summary

Which of these do you know and which can you do?

- I know that animals can move in different ways.
- I know that humans and some other animals have skeletons inside their bodies. Skeletons are made of bones.
- I can observe, compare and describe different bones.
- I know that muscles work in pairs to move a bone.
- I know that exercise makes muscles work hard and that this is good for you.
- I can ask questions and use books, computers and surveys to answer them.
- I can plan and carry out a survey and show my findings in tables, bar charts and pictograms.
- I can look for patterns in tables and graphs.

Complete your **Science Log** to show how well you know these and how well you can do them. Circle a face for each statement.

Glossary

backbone - long bone in the back made from several smaller bones.

bones - hard pieces of the skeleton.

contraction - when a muscle shortens.

contract - to shorten.

grow - to get bigger.

invertebrate - animal without a backbone.

relaxation - when a muscle stretches.

ribs - bones of the chest protecting the heart and lungs.

skull - bone of the head protecting the brain.

spine - the backbone.

muscle - meaty part of body that makes us move.

vertebrate - animal with a backbone.

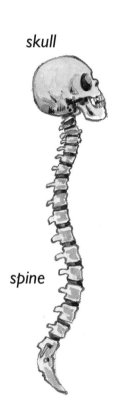

skull

spine

invertebra